I0560924

AMERICAN FANTASY

Second Edition

POEMS BY
STEVEN FAVIANO

Legacy Book Press LLC
Camanche, Iowa

Copyright © 2025 Steven Faviano

Cover artwork and design by Kaitlea Toohey (kaitleatoohey.com)

Illustrations by Nyah Elizabeth Costa

All rights reserved. No part of this book may be used or reproduced by
any means, graphic, electronic, or mechanical, including photocopying, re-
cording, taping or by any information storage retrieval system without the
written permission of the publisher except in the case of brief quotations
embodied in critical articles and reviews.

The views expressed in this book are solely those of the author and do not
necessarily reflect the views of the publisher.

ISBN: 978-1-965602-05-8
Library of Congress Number: 1-14955961078

Dedicated to Mom, Dani, and Dad

TABLE OF CONTENTS

ACT III: DESPONDENCY..55

ACT I:
THE SOCIAL ORDER

THE CANDLE

Fame is a vice and a hoax.
You said to trust this Holy Ghost
beyond the bread and feasible roast –
where did you go when I needed you most?

I believe that someday, sometime,
someone's gonna make a rhyme.
Even we forget the Sun can rise
when there's a reason to be up at night.

I have to run, these hands are too idle,
to me, this is far more than survival.
Maybe someday I can feel safe //
It's not my fault that I'm late
when joy is just a touch away.

Why can't I know the truth?
Tell me why is the Red Sea polluted!
To play a flute for elliptical gods,
is there significance in this small frog?
I pray, I wait, I obey and rebel,
slacking on the corner at the bottom of a well.

I close my eyes to hear it crash,
I'll never get that castle back.
I won't tassel more than I can endure
to feed the beast of doorstep wars.
There's mercy at the end of the sword,
there's power in the extension cord.

There's music in the universe

if only I scribbled down that verse.
At this rate it can't get much worse,
It's fine you missed the baby's birth.

Each seed I grow will corrupt indefinitely,
when I blink, the days shift aimlessly.
It's too late to forgive, too early for apologies,
with no path we have to serpentine –
I can't love you if I can't love me.

I still believe there's hope in us,
identified by what binds us to Earth //
if suspense is the second before the punch,
consider my fist unclutched.
Wield whatever is within your grasp
from finger, pen, final gasp,
the spark reclaimed by palms quick:
the candle has one wick.

CHALLENGER

Becoming in the age of treason
is like swimming without a reason.
With brooch shimmering above the waves,
you stay afloat when your body caves.
Witnessing said struggle above the channel,
polite refusal from note to story,
the current guiding through the coral,
surrender is a quiet victory.
Sensing the riptides encroaching,
unbeknownst to those on the beach,
tenacity divides you from the loach,
you have the strength to be fearless.

IN THE GARDEN

Have we asked the moth if it prefers to drift during day?
Butterflies we won't offer the same, that question is to
remain.
As far as I can say, moths and butterflies flutter the
same;
beautiful in different ways, they light the World when
one's astray.

Around my head the dragonflies, flying faster than my
pen,
soar off the page, dueling till I dot the very ends.
Off my hand the honeybees hover to a blooming leaf,
I observe as they pollinate, they know nectar runs deep.

Exclaiming lines, slicing every 'T', the dragonflies and
honeybees
sting my life and every creed to fill my words with
different needs.
Pluck heartstrings, strum a lovely 'G', the moths and
butterfrees
evolve in diverging beats and come together twice a
dream.

MARKETABILITY

Here is how to feign demand for more supply:
first don your favorite disguise and point
at an isolated place with readily made reprise:
"Those evildoers against our generous sanctions
dare to live willingly within alien agreements!"

Next, mount more hysteria dehumanizing the natives,
as our pockets clang with elegant, rehearsed purse.
"We must protect our neighborhoods here and abroad,
without bombastic reassurance how can business go
    on?!"
(Omit this to the press: we're aligned to either rival.
Remember we can tax them later if it means survival).

Get 10,000 of the freshest, most impressionable helmets
their travel visas and debt forgiveness: It's time to
    venture!
Myself, I have a slick arrangement with a man
whose cartoonishly tall top hat can help funnel in more
camouflaged funding and artillery (honestly, neither
    side should win).

Finally, after tactical persuasion, we get permission to
    interject
from the institutions we dismantled just to resurrect.
"We must restore peaceful glory to those obligatorily
    civil.

It's not our fault their civilization went under,
we just made sunshine indistinct from the thunder."[vw]

[1]For detailed research on the justifications and methodology on US foreign policy, refer to *Manufacturing Consent* by Noam Chomsky (1988).

INDOCTRINATE ME

Left, right, left, right:
each step in sync with the soldier beside.
I can't even vote yet, I've no say in the fight
that's readily here and on the horizon.

I've memorized the maps and commands
to object to the feud between each instructor's land //
Teacher's pet is only satisfied if the Marine –
Florida man who's stuck in the beachheads,
unravels when provoked by parental pushback –
can toy with the young girls and boys
who only seek friends and to enjoy
the meek time remaining in high school.

Left, right, left, right:
it was a calling, a bombing of leadership and skill
that, through space, was seen as incompetent and shrill.
I realized I was walking backwards into Hell –
albeit the warning signs were clear: my body is not for
    sale.
I prophesized like Sergeant Dril:
on to the war crimes, go in for the kill.

CRUCIBLE

Is this the crucible you referred to?
I thought I evolved beyond the requirement
of this harness, this historic feat,
to rise up with victory
against the shackles of humanity.

Have I survived,
or did this torture
force transformation?
I forged and drew this sword
hoping to sheath in their godforbidden heart //
I can and can't remember the face
of the enemy through the fog.

At least I can kneel
in the dust and mud
instead of being the one
to succumb.

SHATTERED

I seize every opportunity
through the fleeting windows
for the rest of the pack, with arms aching,
I haven't done everything yet.

Designated chambers with the bricks stacked,
I shift gears to bounce right back.
The barrier is still too high to grasp,
I switch aim so clear a track: now on the attack.

These walls stand no chance at all,
I pummel the structures down until the whole roof
    collapses!
Now who's laughing? The onlooking competition has
    retracted
as the playing field has tremendously expanded.

DEMOCRACY IN ACTION

Snatch defeat from the jaws of victory –
O' what a twisted irony that the controlled
opposition party relinquishes synergy
with the largest generation of galvanized voters
for the sake of catering to the insurgency,
who, again, have never, never elected them.

Bern'd by the establishment, Swiss in their refusal,
neutral against extremists, bliss in their hollow
  promises //
turned a would-be runaway teal wave into the time-
  tested-and-true
and far-removed policy of:
"Get over it."
as if they give a damn about competing.

It's remarkable that they'd muzzle their own
excitable personas, implementable change,
and of course, any progressive dissent –
at least until HE is back in office,
then suddenly, suburbanites are advocates overnight.

TRIBUNAL

Awhile back, another dreary,
absent was the hopeful's query.
To think a man could resolute
all the things he does refute,
at once voted for the tribute,
and another day ignored the truth.
My God, they yearn for the somber,
their laughter grows with every faulter.

Return to sender
becomes the letter,
the perfect day to furlough.

POLARIZED

There are worse things than betrayal.
How dare you interfere with my scheme
to solidify what remains to become supreme.
I'll demand again: victory is not yours to keep,
as I don't believe in the need to concede.

It's fairly easy with you as my enemy.
There is no middle road, handshakes,
third head to plunder the alienated.
You don't need anyone but me,
we can feud until the country cracks underneath.

Allow me to be blunt - skewering you is plenty fun
and fuels the only motive we've come to love.
Fear of what you can change represents
the first form of unflappable flattery
for the shortest path to neoliberal win.
Any longer, any greyer tomorrows, and I'll quit.

FLOATING HOME

I bore witness as the home where
I sprouted, loved, and raised a family,
floated down the boulevard.

The neighbor's patio is where we stay,
as I couldn't gather the valuables
or stretch these weary legs.
Our home - where the mortgage loan
was placed with all our accolades –
drifted away from the roots we sowed
before engulfing a white picket fence.

Maybe we should have stayed in bed
and dreamt of bluer skies instead.
For now, I'll hold you all tight,
maybe the rainbow will arrive tonight.[2]

[2]While exact numbers vary, approximately 200 million to 1.2 billion
people will be forcibly displaced by 2050 due to the impact of climate
change – citing reports between the United Nations High Commissioner of
Refugees (UNHCR) and the Institute for Economics & Peace.

[UNAVAILABLE]

Hello, my fellow American,
I know this may be shocking to read,
but the Congress has been [censored]
in response to the overwhelming, underfunded,
overprotective [unpermitted] who seek to
completely [censored] our democracy.

Well, your friends here at [redacted]
have been [censored] overtime
scouring through all your [unpermitted],
and found some no-good, anti-establishment
[unpermitted] that really hurt our feelings.
[Redacted] is committed to transparency,
your trust is of [no clearance] importance to us.

That is why you've received this memo via
    [unpermitted]
so if [expurgated] tries to convert you to their
[no clearance], [censored] ways,
we hope you'll return the favor by [censored] us
so [expurgated] doesn't go to [unpermitted]
and you won't be [unavailable].

Verb = [censored]
Noun = [unpermitted]
Place = [redacted]
Pronoun = [expurgated]
Adjective = [no clearance]
Your choice = [unavailable]

WEAPONS OF ABSOLUTE POWER

What is Safe?
Is it at the end of a muzzle uncased
or within the arms of another's embrace?

It's because Safe isn't home,
or at work, or learning in schools,
or when popping corks, praying at church //
It surely isn't on the phone, or at restaurants,
or watching movies, or at brunch.

It's not at nightclubs,
parades, funerals, weddings,
clinics, synagogues, mosques,
sports games, conventions,
car shows, kindergarten, nonprofits,
not in porcelain, rural, or skylines too.

Is knowing this list worse than a bullet?
Fear and money are at the very crux,
and it's because I need to protect us.[3]

[3]The US is the only nation in the world with widespread gun violence,
in part from the fact that there is over 400 million guns in circulation
domestically. Since 2022, gun violence has been the leading cause of death
among children and teens. (Everytown Research & Policy, 2024)

CRISIS

Crisis, crisis, crisis,
crisis, crisis, crisis:
a word catalyzes into meaninglessness.
I pretend that today, a step away
from earthbound face, is plenty safe,
wearing sunglasses in the burnt-out rays.

Am I a fool to be delighted by
what's coming next?
The title is engineered obsolete
because the second I blink,
suddenly we're all falling.

Maybe I should root for serenity
and read aloud in the city streets
what disaster is for me,
as long as we can keep speaking
during the next regime.

A HERO'S REQUIEM

"Chains tethered them to beds," said the overwhelmed
respondent to every fading alarm.
With compassion forced dormant
as rooms naturally for conference, union,
and storage are converted to bind more.

"I can't smoke no more," said she, the charged
veteran that's run out of oxygen again.
With little support, having been escorted
to critical work, tending to the family
of those viciously misinformed.

"Things were different,' said the fresh stranger
checking in whichever room they'd fit.
How difficult it is to be there fourfold -
saving daily lives and witnessing the extinguished -
being told you're doing it wrong
from people lacking empathy and love.

To every pledged Nightingale, your wings
shimmer brighter than anyone else I know.
Your committed care endures from that purity –
thank you, to whom it concerns, for our nurses.[4]

[4]During the COVID-19 pandemic, healthcare workers struggled to provide
adequate care and resources to patients. This is in part due to polarization,
misinformation campaigns, and subsequent demonization of medical
professionals who – on all accounts – are explicitly trained to save lives.
Death itself has no political affiliation.

ONCE IN A LIFETIME

Fell in the morning, the President
spells fortuitous. I can't pay rent
at the moment. Evictions and death,
shoveling shit for overhead markets.

Depreciation, money is hell //
Self-protection, cry in the stairwell.
It's absolution, don't kiss and tell //
Continue to sin: depression for sale.

Enough of the fun, I'm running aground.
Cruising and burning all over town.
Nothing can stop me, a half mile down,
voters spreading and split right on the frown.

Crowding the state, there's no opponents,
Illegal expression, overbearing parents
grouting the coffin. Everyone out, vampires in
that Kamala concoction, the coconut limits.
The power and bliss, light is the crown //
is that a bald eagle in a gown?

The bourgeoisie that powder their nose //
They're all at the same parties, you know.
There's nowhere to go, ran out of blow //
There's no brighter glow for scarecrow
politicians ready to go
than reincarnation or cryogenic holes.

DIPLOMACY

It never ends -
breaking those who refuse to bend,
as austerity turns them to friends
and foes to return again.

Cease your trivial aggression
from my relentless instigation,
and join us to forge a future
liberated from such minute worries.

I'll rendezvous to you
with isle of vivid shadow
to finish what began a century ago.
And with this pact
we can enact
new territory to expand
with and without blood on either hand.

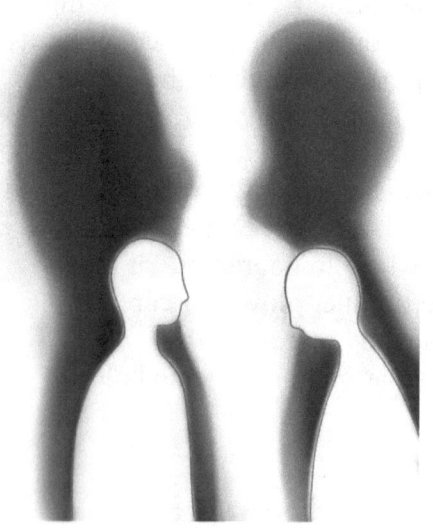

SOUND BITTEN

Let me be clear
to all of those trapped in fear:
while our shared sorrows can't disappear,
let's begin the diminishment today and here.

Know that our odds aren't great,
regardless if you reside in red or blue states.
The system we inhabit thrives in disarray,
so don't forget that love can still trump hate.

Forget about the select decade's war, that
our half-filled homes were founded by crusade,
we must progress with humble gaze
lest we drill blood solely to waste.

I ask not on behalf of the forefathers
but for the safety of our sons, daughters,
still decidings and extra categories,
to unite against these challenges that –
simultaneously – should not go anywhere.

THEATER

Change consumes the stage
before the audience has a say
to burn what has since decayed,
or which direction the globe should rotate.
An auditorium that cannot return
this many tickets that've been punched,
as actors swing whichever way
the wind blows, for their declared estate.

Each byte relies on stage fright
since the lowest denominator is required
for portrayed heights to be embraced
for the "stoic" reaps all the maize.
As the moderator said,
please repeat that again
for sake of dangerous, radical trends,
we profit less from commercial breaks.

KINDLE

Try to swindle the remaining kindle
with swift grip and formidableness,
alas, what sorrow has fell upon
your own dimming twinkle,
that you'd intrude a light show.

Tossed aside as Inferno commands
for treacherous sleight-of-hand:
I truly hope you understand
that without the spark,
you'll perish before the clan.

COMMERCIAL

City streets turned stone cold bleachers,
make a move to take the shot – had enough
of the packaged echo-talk. Do not emulate,
I won't hesitate to peel you open to annunciate.

Take away the money, it's elementary.
Bake enough souffle 'til they fabricate strays.
instead of 40 acres and a mule, take
the opportunity, settle for the fame //
Frame it in a way to get the generation
flocking to the cosmic radiated stage –
do not resuscitate if it comes out of my pay.

I admire how you hustle from the other lane,
no white lighters until I long spawn K-Dot.
I don't discriminate, take some pocket change,
as long as the seats don't have blood clots.
That one's for the industry with bite-sized budgetary,
who make a buck off the blueprint and demand a copy.

WE BRING PEACE

A violin vigil will never be violent;
a traffic stop does not invite a knock;
a sidewalk jog can't end at the cemetery;
a state is wrong to weaponize your car;
It shouldn't be miraculous when they,
free to transition, survive to 35;
kneeling in an empty field is more provocative
than on a convenient, innocent neck.

Breath becomes potent when speaking in mass
or quietly placing the candle in crisp grass.
Chants trend away from the beaten path
to the tune of justice in each progressing step,
all until I look behind to see our
city's perilous vanguard – armed
from charlatans of the Farthest Hill –
surrounded the movement, blocking Main Street
access by way of bullets and tear gas.

A jury of one's peers obviously won't convict
the stand once the judge orders an ovation.
It's hard to change what we can't control,
especially when outrage is undermined
where blossoms continue to rise and rot out of sight.
The Age of Accountability begins,
it's time to Interpol the slave patrols.[5]

[5]Order of references: Elijah McClain, Breonna Taylor, Ahmaud Arbery,
black transgender youth, George Floyd

TODAY

Come for me, let me see
what all the foreseen smoke means
to someone waiting in a tree
for time to reach higher,
Hell can't touch me here.

Plenty seems to be the pre-approved
amount of warnings, bound ties,
and upticks before it was decided
that the world shouldn't be on fire –
I'm so, very, abhorrently tired of climbing.

All around me - above the hindered growth
and encapsulated ash – from this timber skyscraper,
the tallest of all civilization, is a ferocious kind of day.
I feel no reason to boast, they got what they paid for –
as did I, for the apocalypse arrived today.

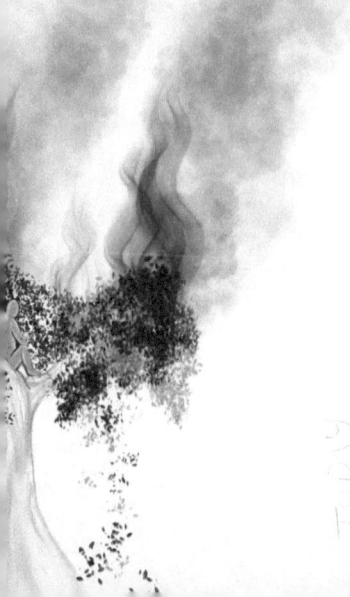

ACT II:
VENTURE

BREACH

In walks Usurper
with prominence in the slither,
through tiny fracture, uninvited,
politely welcomed, and untethered.
It seized our Father
from within walls unflinching,
to transform the permeating war
against devils whose lives mirror ours.
Again assaulted by the hammer drop,
reinforce the cavalry before
it once again departs.

OVER HEAVEN

One believes in gravity –
that necessary imprisonment
to wish upon whatever star
that has fed, died and hence recycled
into nebula dynastinae.

That serenity - whether interest pig or
afflicted armband – impales our shared nature.
This Hell that permeates out of reach,
not in heart or beneath feet,
with gates that rattle in the breeze,
roars as it waits indefinitely.

A conclusive eruption all at once –
palms clench by glimpse of thought –
bow to acknowledged, infinite arch.
There is a chance for redemption
in a second, as the first had fought.

Wings have become obsolete
in a world of decayed technology.
Moving through fingertip universes,
I am alive through chemical enterprise
forbidden to taste or comprehend.

Since dawn fled and arrived before
a shadow was ever witnessed,
Heaven itself became unattainable
as mercy for curious minds:
those endlessly present ponder for
the shortest formula of all humankind.

Memories and identity:
both alone critique the existence
of soul or bone.
Hell cannot be inevitable
or embody justice,
as implied heliocentrism
denies the lives beyond.

Wisdom must exist
on the cusp of here and abyss.
Wandering eyes rival higher judgement,
awestruck by what nothing has become.
Restoring Salvation via assorted memories
with anguish and passion intwined –
I breathe fatigued relief
upon return to my origin.

CURRENTLY

I once wondered about the way water flows.
Wanderlust, I followed the river
upstream to the quiver
of the marching arrow flying north.
Just evenly sheered, I wade in the shallows to be
   genteel.

Each wave that washes over me,
accompanying energy in extravagance that
expose my sins for the salt to seep in:
Water has no consequence.

Whether it erodes,
Pour down in torrent,
catastrophizes s a town,
or relentlessly cascades on this cheek,
I stopped chasing the stream
when I realized all I could be
is adrift –
 I let the current take me.

KETTLE

Create, Conquest, Strife
Three crows that circle over Life.
In order to remove the blight,
I tried conversing with each in flight.

Mocking me, the first lands by my side
to offer something ripe and shiny.
Bewildered as it disappeared again in search
of misery at home and pain to mirth.

The second bird refuses to land
choosing to hover from a distance.
Horizon bound, it circles back,
fearing the grim grasp of the Raven.

The third took bread from my palm,
somehow stoic in the dissonance.
It lingered too long, eyes void of reason,
perhaps it'll leave with the season.

The murder floated there and hearsay,
they smell a feast from afar.
I thought I would join them yesterday,
but I really hate the pecking order.

MARCH TO NOWHERE

Move on, onwards to a better app.
Fuck none, go forward on another path.
Months drain in an instant, we're trapped
in commitment free of blath.

My island erodes with glee
as ships crash, come and flee.
Same situation, a different spring,
I prime what's right, what do you bring?

To settle is to embrace the label,
eggs, bacon, pancakes that match the maple.
Expiration after feasting on the table,
as Plan B is cheaper than a cradle.

All I do is cry in the arms of havoc,
confuse rust for golden brass,
behold the growth of foreign grass
and laugh in the face of epitaph.

RENEGADE

Where have the renegades gone?
It would appear each maven has struck down
their own intended ambitions.
Has each daring effort, more consequential
than the former, forgone a final gasp?

Even as the wind ails, it fails to forbid
the kites from soaring still.
Simple creativity can despoil or enshrine
with regards to monolithic society.

Has the music stopped?
Has the spear finally dropped?
Granted, my two cents won't be enough
to keep the lights on.

CLIMBING

I rest my chin on the side of the building
neck outstretched to the stars,
blabbering to the reverend
that I don't need prayers,
a hero or villain.

What's the difference in power
between these scaffolding towers?
I can't compete with giants without
building the strength to keep climbing.
I've been thinking for hours
about the view from power,
just a glimpse of the accomplished -
I'll make it home Mom, I promise.

These clouds are impeding my judgement,
I can't see through the fog.
How much further to the top?
When's too late to stop?

LOOK AWAY

How I wish to avert my gaze
from all the crimes against the human race,
prohibition of creation, outlawing emancipation,
death for existing in time and space,
the freedom to choose macabre faces.

I can't, I can't look away:
It's history in motion; it's change as it's made.
To pretend like our condition to anticipate first
the utter defeat, cruel victory, decisive dwelling,
all in the name of humanity.

I can't look away.
it's my compulsion
to compose what I see
and be who I believe.

GHOST TOWN

Outsider waltzing by blushed shine
wheeling that shanty, torn arc
across this vaster half –
The Wind is prohibited.

Earnest, benign, regalia aside,
I contest to be bitter or petrified
by the amount of absent vines
that fetter the doors and canopies.
Had they known better, spoiled fruit
is surely within spitting distance.

It's hard enough to holster resolve
when you can't contend to lose it all.
The Dust confessed to being involved,
judging by this tumbling wanderer.
I can't pretend the Air dissolved:
swivel-head, extra lead, penicillin, exit plans.

I considered it all – even controlled how long
it'd take the shells to fall,
so there should be a shimmer
for each touch of crawl.

COALMINE CANARIES

Oh, what to sing
in the bronze cage?
We may hear a rhythm
from the gathering heartbeat.
A song that we, aimless canaries -
dispersed morning rays -
can retreat in serenity.
Little tweets
trapped in paranoia,
infatuation,
cry for resuscitation.

FALLING FORWARD

I'm feeling free when on that grind,
at my best working over-time.
I leave the nest when the time is right,
on my own to fall and catch the wind in-flight.
The songs that chime from tuning trees
vibrate every fiber from head to knees,
I catch the intended glimpse with eyes wide shut,
trust when you fall that I'll pick you right back up.

DECLARATION

"I can move mountains!"
Declared a forestine being
from the foot of frothing obstacle
scraping higher than the sky dared to climb.

An all-beholding endeavor to approach
and place palms on formidable pillar,
with such a declaration
that pines would skirt and uproot.

First the shade began to split,
incinerating as the land recoils //
Crisp wind assaults our lungs
as avalanches mist upon fall.

And thus, the colossus decidedly adjourned.

MIRROR

It started at the mirror.
I tried to see past the other guy.
he looked back not so sure,
I extended wings so he could fly.
 His hair was long, his time was short,
I felt the same as if in court.
He pretended to not be stuck in a box
but all he could do was charade along.

I put my hand up to the glass
and met the coolness of his palm.
We had a second of a connection,
yet he was stuck in that dimension.

Why was he there, I wondered.
Was he waiting for his life to pass?
I went ahead to close the light,
the stranger remained in the past.

BE YOURSELF

I could and will do more,
but it's not my life to explore.
I believe each of your reports,
those sinister twisters seek only to destroy.[6]

I want you to know
I love who you are and I adore
your many shades and thoughts,
your shoes and makeup too.

Those clothes can't zip around my torso,
please let me say before you go onstage:
you deserve every ounce of support as
Sophie's dreams granted splendid rapport.

Mary Moon reclaimed her star,
now it's up to you and our united enclave.
Trust me when I say to trust yourself,
show the world you're more than just brave.

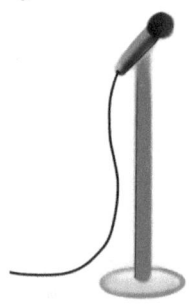

[6]With hundreds of legislative bills directed to alienate and persecute
LGBTQ+ individuals across the U.S., it is all the more crucial to support
and protect those within the community.
If you or a loved one in the LGBTQ+ community are struggling, please
contact the Trevor Project at (866) 488-7386.

DRIVEN

Roll them down, feel the breeze.
climate control so you won't freeze.
We can pull over if you need
to breathe away from the antics of me.
You can walk home on the streets like an addict.
The Christmas stuff's still in the attic,
so why bring up old shit?

If you needed some help
why didn't you ask for some when
it was happening? Why go through it again?
It's not time for an argument,
all of my gas money's been spent
and I'm not fucking with rent.
Nobody made you hell bent,
take a second to catch your breath
and stop pestering me about stale bread.

The cop didn't even see when I sped.
I'm already ahead with hindsight in vision.
God didn't give you permission
to have such malicious intentions.
I've been this way since conception.
I'm braking.

BRACE YOURSELF

Maintain eye contact.
The parade on display,
in disarray as the drivers relax.
Bring up the contract
with red ink splattered
across all dotted lines.
Don't call from the back,
climb up and reclaim
tattered patriarch for risk's sake.
Erased roads those crossers know,
ready the head, cushion the blow.
Impact.

WAYFINDER

Glass shattered as the bar closed that night.
where there's smoke, there's fire //
meet where the sky and horizon impasse.
I taste crimson as the shards trespass.

Where are my roots? I'm broken by the stem.
When I'm charred and bruised, can you tell who I am?
I can shut my eyes if I land in the bin.
My friend, can you help me understand
if I am Hell or whether I am Man?
Adrift, the creek carries me to the pier,
did the rivers scheme to intersect?

I stand when I land back on Earth.
Tyranny can't dispel my smirk,
any more than frictional traditions slow mirth,
all while they insist I resist our history.
Now, breaking waves, my hands steer the mast
attached to sails tattered by wrath.
We need the wood; timber can't be ash.
I've broken the wheel, down with the caste.

When sand once again coils around our feet
and it's critical to disturb that peace,
the Stars advise that if one were kind,
Tangaroa would wrestle back the tide.[7]

[7]In Māori and Polynesian culture, Tangaroa is the god of the sea, protecting the ocean, rivers, and all life within the waters. He is immortalized with the saying: "Tiaki mai i ahau, maku ano koe e tiaki" ("If you look after me, then I will look after you").

LUCKY STREAK

A spark, ignited by uncertainty
and enflamed by a compulsion
to torch my own road,
ricocheted on oblivious barriers.
The western endeavor consumed
the fumes in my gas canister,
it took short talks at pit stops
to convince the reflection
that the journey is worth it.

One break, a simple handshake,
an apartment furnished on the river basin,
a succulent deal wrapped in tenderized steak,
all began from some mistake that
brought all this abundance to my gape.

I could never recognize cloaked blessings
when they disappeared from sight.

It took all my might, all the light
that glimmered in stranger's eyes,
the stolen time from exploitative jobs,
and a belief that luck's on my side,
for each day to perfectly catalyze
so today I could realize that I have arrived.

OBSESSION & RESISTANCE

I've done it.
After toiling and brewing
and crafting and sitting
restlessly at this office desk,
months upon hours of pondering
and soiling the blank page,
I've started,
and I can't do it.

There's a grand diner opening,
there's a salary to be made,
there's my dog to walk,
there's all day tomorrow,
and I just stare at the outline.
I'll reward myself with starvation,
I'll yearn for a blow of inspiration.

It's already begun,
rose, fell, and climaxed
while imprisoned in this head.
It's already done,
as it arrived and fled,
and the ink continues
to run on ahead.

CONVENTIONS

For the chorus:
social norms are carefully crafted
shackles for your everyday usage.
What would happen
when we're all cut loose,
collectively conscious, severed from the illusion?

My stanzas flow to make sense
of this dense, societal fortress.
I join the ride and the scheme,
though I have no need
for structure or rhymes,
which is apparently the theme.

To write is to improve this fortitude,
only the poets[8] would dare attempt
to dismantle every convention.
Even if I sell out,
you won't know how I felt,
my only desire is creation.

[8]"Only the poets" refers to a speech by activist-writer James Baldwin,
"The Artist's Struggle for Integrity" (1962)

OVERHAUL

Anyone can paint,
there's no standardized canvas.
Everyone muddles over sacrificing that
sacred stillness, to disrupt serene purity.

Disassemble to reconstruct
the life you've endured.
Putting ink down to paper
is too risky if not perfect.

The Artist requires the volition
to destroy that false dichotomy.
To chisel away the softened clay
is the first step to create.

DREAMER

We found a way to a magical place, land free
of horrors its very leaders pave.
It's been this way for centuries –
no matter what we gave
or what language I speak –
here you will stay if you behave.

Displacement for Little Green Men
first as slaves, depraved
from ships to pavement.
Then the definition changed,
so system updates are made
to accept migrants with exploitable
fire of a better life.

When the worshipped clouds
suddenly rain bombs instead of relief //
o' the humanity lost means to flee
to love and hatred, a far-away community.
How quickly passed the Darién Gap
and for decades, toiling in the shattered
construct, hot fields that for pennies entrap
the most deportable just to feed everyone else.

You can make it here, and anywhere, know please
los inmigrantes construyeron este país.

REVISIONS

Of all of my revisions made -
spelling erorors and butchered mistakes,
some from missounding similes,
others that border on make believe -
I take time to pause
to dream of a thought
of a growing idea planted within me
reminded of the branching tree.
A shot at the insanity,
I pinpoint with more precision.
When I feel the rough draft encroaching in,
I erase the run-on synonyms.

ACT III:
DESPONDENCY

ON BEHALF OF FASCISM

"It's an infestation!" yodeled the Mold,
from deep inside a broken home,
who's hope for repairs, cars or healthcare,
along with any chance to resist, or interject,
was smothered out long ago.

The Mold declared: "Shut the door on this interloper
so this roach can't flee or interfere.
No, don't look away from him, or her, or whatever,
I've decided that they deserve my fear.
We won't need their categories anymore.
You know they shouldn't be trusted, just sign here."

"Is this what it's supposed to look like?
Present something better next time.
Pathetic – your nuisance is noted
and the minute continues to crawl,
use this to immortalize your bravado –
every gaze you meet will now cast a shadow."

"It threatens our existence! Our very work and
    traditions,
all that slaving away in utter agony and disarray.
Defend yourself at any cost; it's using words again…
did it mention it has personal constitution?
Prepare for a new world without these strays,
to care for creatures is to play pretend."

"The regime's preference: they can't work, so they
    won't eat.

This marked menace must be removed,
away from eyesight or buried with their own kind.
The Exterminator Parade marches on this beat,
stamping 'innocents' with their grooved boots.
Pay their desperate cries no mind."

"How is this our fault?
We were inspired by orders to distinguish,
persecute, and eradicate any and all
members from that designated group.
It's not me – I watch TV and voted
for those who made this possible."[9]

[9]While genocide does not require authoritarianism, mass human rights
violations take place under such policies. Complacency is the breeding
ground for violence to occur.
For more information on ethnic cleansing or genocide, please visit sources
such as the Holocaust Memorial Trust at hmd.org.uk/learn-about-the-holo-
caust-and-genocides.

LIFE RAFT

My dearest Life Raft,
with safety shimmering off your mast,
far above me, where the waves crash,
hold fast. I reach out just to grasp
the bubbles swirling from my mouth clasped.

I'm not a drowned one yet
with memories I've tried to forget.
What's weighing me down is the reckless
need for a second chance.

Deeper still, muscles furloughing to relax
as I tremble, peddling against the dark
maw of whatever's swimming next
to me. I think it just touched my leg.

I might close my eyes to rest –
maybe I'll wake up refreshed
and back in the nest. Perhaps that's a guess.
Maybe later I, alone, can swim back
with clearer head so we can be together again.

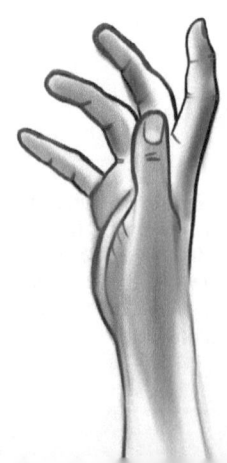

THE VOID DOESN'T CARE

How should I cope with that unwavering,
nihilistic, endless night sky?
We're spinning through void uncontrollably,
where did we come from, where are we going?

I know of stars that we haven't reached yet,
I've heard of Gods that no one's even met,
I felt the fire and wished it were wet,
I've learned that the world is somehow in debt.
I own three pairs of the same sweatpants,
I've powered through when I was depressed,
I can't shower without my anxious pet,
I've bought a bookshelf to cover with plants.

I guess this is why I write,
to feel complete with a puzzle inside.
Self-awareness is such a plaited curse,
all we know is from somebody else's words.

ESCAPE THIS PLACE

Take me away.
It's easy, I don't hesitate
to erase the pain
by bending ink.
Flexible, nimble grace
pick the place and time
that esquire can interject.

I don't feel a thing.
More colors, enough upheaval,
skin is prettier when sketched pink.
This booth is not the end of me,
this art is not temporary,
this imprisonment isn't one to seek,
I'm trapped in memories that won't flee.

NO THANKS

A colleague, peering from over shoulder,
inquired with a brusque overtone:
"You should make your poems shorter,
these are treacherous for me to read."
So I replied with no surprise:
"No thanks, Tony. Go, fuck off
to your boring, bland desk
featuring pictures of places
that you won't ever visit."

JOYRIDE

Every travel time feels so lonely,
preference could even be
with a companion sleeping.
Backed up, can't the flow let go,
each day I forget
which way is home.

AWAY

I haven't claimed a better place,
but if I wait, I doubt you'll feel the same again.
They say every moment should be savored.
They say to not displace your feelings.
In this giving space, it's hard to know what's to take,
I need courage for what to say.

I'll run away from everything that makes me happy.
– I should relinquish some strength
and hold my brain for decisions without delay.
Façade aside, do I have what it takes?

I stay away, it's safer than holding sap trees.
Emotions away, I can't pretend to know the craze,
be it mine, or whatever's trending on the fade.
Contact's a ride, I am the one that they have waited.

I'll pull away from the truth of what you tried to
    portray.
I'm scared it means that we share the intimate
vulnerability that we both crave.
If I jump over shade and make home a place
for honesty, love for commitment's sake,
would you stay? Or are we stuck in space?

IGNITION

Crackling under the summer night,
with no retreat from envy leaves,
smoke billows over light
dreams release from detached trees.

Stagnant twigs snap to relax,
change consumes barbaric armor,
a flicker born from ash
ignites with tremendous vigor.

Yet all I see is haze in sprawl
that settles between us.
This snow isn't natural,
there're voices in the wind gust.

The stars, they hide.
Suffocated out, the lights reside.
Into the pond we dive
to find safety in the abyss.

In trading one fantasy for another,
we've survived Dante's embrace
as my mind goes blank.
My pillow is my only lover.

DESOLATE PIONEERS

A wasteland envelops aureate boots,
who groveled all the while:
"This damned quicksand never
coagulates during the day,
not when regal Sun stretches
and coughs on divine land."

The teardrops crumbled long ago
as the bumbling, disgruntled warrior
scorched remaining bridges between
sought product and home.
"These damned animals
lost all gratitude for us pioneers,"
said through the crooked tooth,
charging through a neighborhood
systematically rooted in marsh and pollute.

BAGGAGE

I'm more tired
than I thought I was.
We're staying out too late
the longer that we play,
the night, we overcame.
Except the bottles that we drank
bring out love in different ways.
Simplify it all, you say that like I'm wrong,
How am I to blame when you're snuffing out the flame?
Do I need to drag this burden every time we leave the
    plane?

OPEN DOOR

I saved enough paper for
nothing more than a cheap vacation
for us to roll to, posted at door,
ready to move or hibernate.
I know you've been busy too.
It's the best we can do.

You said I deserve better
than a shabby man with bed head,
who rips holes in the ceiling fan
when it's too loud for morning rest.
Even though we both agreed
this lease was temporary.

Believe me, I know I owe you
more than what we've gone through.
We fuck on the garden gate
while neighbors complained from their estate,
now court's involved from your mistake,
at least our bones ain't ache.

Is it enough if I've saved up
all the notes you left on
the kitchen fridge, the nightstand,
every time when you were pissed
at the circumstance we were in.
Because the door is open, but who's leaving?

NO SOULS

Where did you go?
In this city of millions
thriving in perpetual limbo;
I embrace you with certainty
that it's okay to feel alone.

Why feel the need to reach?
Professing to strangers of lore
in hope that they will be
the one you're searching for.
When in reality
they're not the type to pour.

After months of defeat
of moving mountains over borders:
"You don't belong to me."
"It's not like you called me yours."
If this is how it's supposed to be,
don't turn around when walking out the door.

You reflect in each piece
from the perspective of the floor:
What does love mean to me?
Is it even worth fighting for?
And yet you choose to bleed:
why not remove the sword?

DUELING FATES

The Bull has no need for meat or bone,
as a formidable machine that never falters
Right hook, left slightly better,
whose stride unimpeded,
challenges every single gazer.

The Matador is skin and soul alone,
a crimson artist who teeters on the rink.
Hopes lighter than a feather,
whose courage exists as instinct,
remains too stoic for his own good.

The battle, the show, the political arena!
Should the Matador prevail, he's in the endgame
as the Bull's fate nonetheless remains the same.

VIOLENCE

I was gifted with this heartbeat
to grow in strength and keep pace
with Hermes, whose heat
is the tether between them and me.

It's ablaze – each impulsive breath
that catalyzes into steam is marked
by the beast, as I tremble in the sand
believed once to be holy land.

Fight! Fight like all of mankind
rests upon your shoulders to rise!
I don't know how to occupy my time.
My task – crucial as the Priest had deemed –
is to listen and liberate in accordance with
the man standing a year older than me,
who's commanded by that unbroken order.

I never questioned why the recruit
with evicted legs is refused
the benefits that would repair his life
How I wish an innocent snakebite
could ruin me just enough to be sent home
in a cushioned seat, not wrapped in cloth.

Was this accident supposed to happen – to sever
me from our cross-country convoy?
Eventually I remember even begging Allah
that if my soul is cold, bury me
how I should be normally, not left
as a statistic like so many, many before.

Here I remain – free at home, at last,
to wander around broken gazebos:
the open breeze, no magazines, right to occupancy.
I don't know if my old heroics were
ever told to the trickle-down gun,
whose quota turned my 13 stripes vertical.[10]

[10]Despite having a military budget that surpasses the next 11 nations combined – over $850 billion – the United States has roughly 32,000 veterans experiencing homelessness amid increasing socio-economic inequality that affects millions of Americans.
It is estimated that to address the homelessness crisis in its entirety, it would take between $11 billion and $30 billion.

WILDFIRE

I don't need your permission
to run amok by personalized fission.
Forget about every catching up,
I've decided to scorch the very earth;
either join or get out the way.

Any nascent who can break astray,
who sees the path before its made,
collected just to fade, the wind
carries our worries farther than light admits.

For next time, again, we'll have to wait,
remember to bury each intention in ash.

FRUITION

So you've settled down
with your crooked ambition
because your friends quit coming to town
and the despair came to fruition.

Night has fallen and it's quite the shame
that your emotional tuition
has shriveled from playing games,
has your hope become extinguished?

Holding yourself up on the bathroom sink
and hardly recognize your own reflection.
You punch the glass until your hand is pink,
it got the better of your intuition.

As the morning breaks
with the swelling heatwave,
the new day demands you awake
and allow yourself time for creation.

SEMINAR

Oh no,
here comes the desolate cloud
spiraling down from their
post-morning seminar,
and yet again, with
anguish looming
over shoulder,
I said nothing
as the books
fell from
her bag.

All her secrets.
All her being.
Vanquished over
a night initially believed to be in her means.

Now, she lays there,
amid more threats of harm,
assault, and hatred.

She is safe with community,
she is safe with protection,
she is safe when she is believed.[11]

---

[11]According to the National Sexual Violence Resource Center, one in 5
women and one in 16 men are sexually assaulted while in college, with
more than 90% of assault victims on college campuses going unreported.
Comparatively, 63% of national sexual assaults are not reported to police,
with around 1% being reported lead to conviction.

WEIGHT

I don't like cigarettes,
I detest the smell and taste.
I enjoy the sensation at least
once the nausea evaporates.
Remove the market from my lungs.
They either act cool or falsify enticement, never both.
Like a Bond-type on the casino floor
or the overworked nursing student.
That's their vice that feels wrong but looks right
as you have yours, and I with mine.
It's like teetering on a bridge
or strolling in a forest fire.
We all carry that weight.

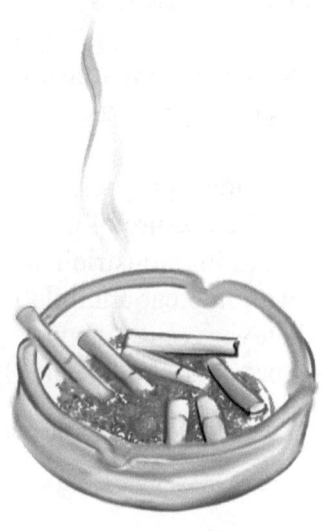

EXTINCTION

The last white rhino died today[12]
after evolving far past his prime,
after invaders stole the sublime ivory from
Sudan's blood brothers, cousins, soul sisters,
 and hung on a chandelier above a swooning mistress.

A mountain of bison skulls resides
high above the local tribes, crying
by the sight of millions once enshrined,
then destroyed as they fight to survive
from settled men, smiling for causing the plight.[13]

Mighty tigers, reduced to twenty-five-foot zoos,
imported in hundreds, skinned for tapestries and rugs
    too,
with no space to escape, more live in one southern state
than exist across the entire continent of Asia,
and can't return once domesticated.

In this speck of specks of recorded history
includes Sumer, the Giza Pyramids, knockoff
    Pantheons,
religion of today, Crusades, plagues, colonization,
the Qing, the Queen, the erasure of misdeeds,
revolution after revolution, industrialization,
a steady stream of war, nuclear annihilation,
the Internet and whatever comes next.
All we know exists between the Ice and Space Ages.

[12]In March 2018, the last male northern white rhino named Sudan passed
away at the age of 45.
[13]In the 1800s, nearly 60 million bison were killed as a tactic to decimate
Indigenous populations.

MENAGERIE

The two exiled down the river
from their false start, both shiver
as the final gambit fades from shared cave,
illuminated. Laughed while feeling saved,
reanimated until dragged back to the grave.

Hello, my loving foe.
I'm alive beneath the bone, no suodiu.
Sheathed becomes the beak,
tethered I lay and watch as you feast.
Like criminals, smooth or bitter,
evicted liver at the place where waves
are torn down from support pillars.
Drole vulture kettles, an angel
come to deliver me of turmoil.

Receipt of fortune fell away yesterday,
the powerful duel portrayed in the flames.
Deceit is for devils lassoed, demons
defeated the day Hell turns cold.
On the uptick, nostalgic of February
when sweet wine danced in charades.

Love opened up the gates,
games are meant to play,
opinions mutate like flu,
how could I do that to you?

GRIEVING

One foot in, one out
of the grave that holds our dearly
beloved and now departed,
who's ecstasy for the little things –
sidewalk flowers, sunlight on his face,
the stars, what people bring –
has extinguished.

He once drifted this way,
delicately, like a comet, from outer space,
only to soar by those with outstretched hands
who could look, reach high, but can't grasp,
as his trajectory went from great heights
to settle in the crater on a bench.

I'll always remember the joy on his face the
moment he realized he was safe.
I recall the indiscriminate love he possessed,
without judgement, but people-pleasing, yes.
I'll never forget the day when his doubts overcame
his mindfulness and the world became an earthquake.
I let go of the man formerly a part of my life
for betraying himself and embracing strife.

Is he alright? What is he doing now?
Does he have enough air in the casket?
Did he dig himself out without our knowledge?
Has he grieved the loss of me and that tired version of
  himself?

Were the dozens of people that believed in his truth,
with intention of inviting him inside, simultaneously
    have
the revelation that who he was couldn't come back?

Like a snake that sells its shed skin
to be used in belts, boots, and vests,
it pleases share this tale from
the perspective of those who once loved and lost you.

INSOMNIAC

Shadow-basked eyes
remain after sleepless days
and wired moonlight.
Take it back,
the moment's over.
It's dead, it's done with,
the watch is gone
and the time won't return.
It refuses to,
after barters and prayers riddled
into shins.
I forgot
where the car is parked.

PROLONG

I thought I was wrong
to belong with someone who
held me so tightly, all through
the nightmares of wicked, split tongue.
I should have steered clear
instead of infecting another lover
with hollow promise not to suffer,
this isn't the day to recover.
I'm sorry that Mars fell down,
sorry that I'm not someone else,
that I said I would be stronger,
not prolonged, but thanks
for the hope anyway.

DARKEST POND

I don't remember who I saw
as my eyes adjusted to the darkest pond.
Charred, soured by inhumane hours
that dredged the forever, endless night.
How long did I search within
for any sign of justification
of the discussion I had with said abyss
that stretched a mere two meters in width?

Nearby, toppled was evidence of the empire,
praised and sullied before rightfully destroyed.
I have no blood in what transpired,
yet I barely fathom such horrors.
I'll ask again for His forgiveness
as I peeked, I prayed that they finally rest.
Across the world we beg to cease hostilities,
I looked the deepest, and
found no excuse for its existence.[14]

[14]Located in Auschwitz-Birkenau concentration camp – the site where 1.1 million of primarily Jewish civilians were systematically persecuted and killed –ponds and rivers became stained black as a result of the nearby crematoriums. The scale of devastation from genocides like the Holocaust cannot be understated and is incomprehensible to adequately grasp. In the US, far-right lawmakers have banned and subsequently are trying to erase invaluable stories that provide historical context – including the Pulitzer Prize-winning graphic novel, Maus by Art Spiegelman, in 2022.

ACT IV:
ALCHEMY

FOOLISH

Naysayers claim I'm too reckless,
reluctant to set roots,
dimmer still with new tools,
too careful on the edge.

I rock upon this cliffside
as its fate to gleefully recite.
If I belong to the rapids below,
that remains to be persuaded.

My testament throughout the light
with ecstasy in a dance, turmoil,
I'm here, I'm free, I do as I command,
I join this journey hand-in-hand.

DIVINATION

It arrived right on time
as I recall, as I prophesized,
that I'd wield the talesmen of my own
might, this intervention was guided.

With studious, ridiculous, zealous,
blasphemous attempts to manifest
this list – with pyre burning every fingertip –
it fled as I released and still came back to see me.

Fleeting hope and vanquished fears
decline to interfere, it's known that I steer
poised, raised, and averted smite:
I declare this life to be mine.

SOOTHSAYER

Hindsight is deprived of the warning signs
from the higher field respective to the foreseer.
Runes, when cherished enough to leave
the message perplexed, can reveal more
about your perspective than just the future.

What is this sensation?
It's as if my instincts aligned to who
I always hoped to arrive as.
Healthy, happy, and accepting of
the journey to graze the sky
and kick off the valleys.

It can take a lifetime, generational support,
or the instantaneous impulse to just start.
If intuition – not bound in religion, echoes
of judgement, or only travesty on the horizon –
gnaws at your spirit until you grant kindness,
patience, and above all collaborate,
then follow your heart,
for once,
for yourself,
and for fucks sake.

Make no mistake: destiny unfolds
as the tide craves to erode stable shore,
it's up to us – together with this present –
to assemble a diverse, resonate world.

EMPEROR

Begin again demands the cycle,
whose voracious flame,
sneered command, and ancient name
assured the turning of the battle -
left vacant by the holy toll,
cut short by tenacious spear,
and reflected on the bronze shield.
Who awoke the sinner
from the den of its' brethren?

HIEROPHANT

Much to your dismay,
I am the second to reach the peak.
Call it a quest, call it perseverance,
call after I awake with a chai latte
to apologize for compromised subtlety.
I am brusque – not dull or sloth – I
forbid that language from your truth.
Granted, this is far away from my
comfortable nest, where the wisest vines
entangle every appendage down,
yet I stride with enough formidability
to trample any loathsome party.

TWINNING

You've certainly heard
of how I've prospered today.
> Oh you haven't?
> Well you'll learn.
Essentially, in the shortest sense,
basically what had happened was –
> you'll love this, I'm grateful
> you're a great listener –
I decided to try and find this medallion
forbidden, hidden somewhere in the attic.
> I shouldn't rummage around there,
> the spiders can be quite sporadic.
So I carefully, meticulously, brazenly
plunged myself into each and every square.
> I guess they're more like cubes,
> but anywho, I scoured througout the
> evening.
I wasn't scared – okay so the crawlers
needlessly gave me the heebie-jeebies –
> I stopped and stared because of the
> uncovered.
> It was there! Smack-dab residing on
> the family album.
The sheen wasn't pristine, granted I
remembered it from my childhood dreams.
> But the coat was ivory, I adored the
> pressings,
> it must've been mint if the grime
> wasn't dressing.

Then, get this, you won't believe what I did next.
I brought it back down, toiled away at something else,
set it somewhere in the house, can't
find it, and now I need your help.

MOONCHILD

Here it comes again.
That longing for the crucified
to see mist in either eye,
be healed because your life is sewn to mine.

Your perception mixes with the dreams
as nobody else has witnessed.
Don't you dare take this kindness
for granted; if it's broke I'll try to fix it.

You can't owe me one.
Take it back, that's enough
forgiveness that scrapes my back.
It's a loving letter that I
can't bear to send yet.
Let the dive commence.

DANDELION

Your yellow mane grows farther
over yonder with proper fertilizer.
There's no need to inflame or
shrink when you're tenderized.
Stand fast on sacred ground,[15]
the monsoons can't batter you down.
Reach out, breathe pollen in,
glow bright with sunlight on your skin.
I refuse to believe
that you'd wither without me.
You grow stronger with every heartbeat,
inhale and you'll start blossoming.

[15]"Stand your sacred ground" references professor-author Brené Brown's
book, *The Gifts of Imperfection.*

THE HERMIT

Head down,
no breaks,
you better dribble.

Wear the crown,
or a cape,
finish your scribbles.

Do not drown,
try to moderate,
leave no detail abysmal.

Wisdom sought
through fierce solitude,
illuminated in such a way
which pierced my lantern's cage
and expelled it's very shadow.

FORTUNA

Luck within my wrist
exists without hesitation,
prohibiting the turn
from freedom to secure,
cursed with phantasmal bliss.

Thus permits the hourglass,
stoic in static and half
content with its fill,
disaster precedes fruition
as the ash smolders still.

JUSTICE

Let the sword gently sever the binding
between the split of forbidden fates.
She refuses to know which direction
her spit may land, instead can sense the imbalance
that shifts the curvature of her hand.

The assault against the fragile scale
of a singular crow, with attempt to elongate
a shriek that drowns the very tales
that the heart of Justice seeks to palpate.

To delegitimize this history
is to reject peace in entirety.
Bring up such untimely truth
to weigh against the lying brute's.

STAGNATION

You can be patient
or take a leap of faith.
Wait for the obstacle's downfall
or jump higher, mightier with strength
you didn't know you can conjure.

Doesn't it get sour - the savor of
wasted hours staring up at the scaffolds
stretching to heights you haven't tried to climb?
Take a fresh breath, it's okay to unwind and
step back, the view says you're on the right track.

You can soar, you can trace sky vapors,
you can lay in the grass as moss gathers
on that terrible tower; Fear has so much power
when you remain in place, an observant person
can always find a way towards grace.

If every moment before was clouded in hesitation,
then you're prepared to sever the decayed twine,
to be released with every fiber of your ambition.

CURSE

You said a man could pass by my gaze,
so I walked politely and dropped my shades.
To avert my smirk from crumbled glance,
to witness change as they usurp,
all for this god forsaken earth.
.
Starting today, I begin my curse
peering out the window, I clutch my purse
seven car lanes behind your hearse.

TEMPERANCE

What's with the stars in the sky,
with their lack of faltering eyes?
They encourage us to look up and wonder why
while we lay on the hood of my car,
imagining what other planets are like.

It's the same night you showed over tears,
that you shared with me all your cosmic fears.
All I could do was listen and hear
as we fell down the rabbit hole of despair.

I tell you there's nothing wrong with holding back
when we're animalistic, or under attack,
so our bond doesn't shatter or crack,
but we all know, it's connection that we lack.

I say that it's alright, the sky won't collapse today,
society might, so BMW take us away.
At least we've got lust to answer our prayers
and to fool us into living up, life's not a feint affair.

GROUNDED

I defy gravity up the ladder,
way past Everest, did I reach my peak yet?
Remind me to ask my network
if I fall, to ensnare me in the web
or at least lay down a mattress.
I can't see.
Why is there smoke and mirrors
here in the stratosphere?
Now I only float in zero G's.
Now I get to catch the sunset eternally.
Now can someone play piano for me
so I don't drift away from time and peace?
I feel the words running from my brain
so much so that the language has escaped.
Do you see me?
Am I too high in the blue crumb?
From here I can see all of the cities,
and squish them between index and thumb.
How do I get grounded?
In a spectacular ball of fire and fury?
Will you wish for my return trip?

THIS BLESSED PLACE

The palace I envision
rests on the mountainous impasse,
see how regal the staff upon the flag
shimmers, two halves of the solstice.
I hear the walls crumble
as it shakes the pavement from miles away,
blessed be each and every particle
as the waves collect in mass.
Feel the weight upon my shoulders
as burden grips both collar bones.
Who would've known that
sand shifts quicker than the boulder.

REBEL TO THE CAUSE

I'll take a breath and get this off my chest:
why do y'all stress when I've taken the flagship?
Like a hooded bird, I did it just because I could,
not third, but first as all victors should.
Taking time and making pace, I won't rub it in your face.
It's not a race, but I won, tell the men to make quicker haste.

Let's take it for a spin, not that there's anything left to win,
once a revolution I make amends to cut loose ends.
Now on the high seas baring that delightful Pisces,
is there enough room for us to seize?
I'm sure there's someone out there for me,
we'll just have to sail and see.

NIGHTSHADE

The truth is a bit excessive
for someone set in calumny.
to regress from any forgiveness,
there're plenty forgiveness left in the deep end.

Bella said you don't sleep very well there,
Bella said you've scribbled plenty since the tyrant.
Let me guess: your howls have attracted
exactly what you've beckoned for,
the lie is you recognized what was in store.

I assume nothing, I'm devoid of those illusions,
I attest that illuminated nights have me reeling,
eyes locked on whatever's behind the ceiling.
Perhaps I want to rest too much, I've been
overindulging on all the sheep that run across.

There's the Hat Man in the corner –
with the burden of another news monger
exclaiming that the world is in grave disorder.
Tit-for-tat: paving each nightmare as normal.

SUNSHINE

"Hello again"
said Happiness to all her plants,
"you've certainly flourished since
I've last come around to this side.
How sublime! You've dedicated more
time to enjoy yourself outside.
Awaken, I adore how you grow
and synthesize in the early lights.
Postponed no more, gaze upon all
you've done since yesterday.
My dear, I've never left.
Speak aloud without critical acclaim
that you are worthy of every ounce of love,
like an overflowing chalice with your name
inscribed on the inside."

JUDGEMENT

A bullet could bounce this way
in the whisper of tomorrow's pitiful news.
Asleep at the wheel, reins remain steadfast
by grip of both life and death.
Fate may bestow this with absence of
grovel, prayer, technician or insight.

And they were all targets
of permeating violence of the mind;
scarcity, isolation, disillusionment,
an overdose on podcast pills
and projection.

The word christened by God at the instant
she looks up and sights a star,
becomes a chapter's phantom
obliterated in elliptical design,
as the cycle perpetuates for generations.[16]

---

[16]Note from the author: Fate brought you to this moment, somehow and
some way. In whatever cosmic order looks down upon humanity – the
potential for mass violence, authoritarianism, and inequality – you have
agency to make positive change. It's easy to be passive and complacent,
absorbing whatever comes your way. Make no mistake: whoever you are,
you influence the world around you – just as there are horrors, people can
be surprisingly beautiful. How did you show up for yourself today?

JUPITER

Ganymede roosts on Zeus' shoulder,
sharing secrets from the new world order,
that half the planet is getting hotter
and the rest of it is underwater.
The titan replied while averting his eye,
and a glance of horror peeled over the sky,
a snap of thunder would set it in order
to halt crawling violence, negligence, and war.
Yet he relaxes, sights on the horizon,
the darkest night reaps higher harvest.
Aphrodite's shield shimmers in twilight,
Nike in fist, humanity is victorious.

THE SATURN TAX

I confess //
Despite the rigid infamy possessed by
our internal parents demanding to stress
inner children who yearn for the sun's bliss,
growing old means you are responsible to dress.

Karma comes and all I want to do is hide in trees,
drama collides with open eyes; I cry when stung by
  honeybees.
My mantra tries to convince me that the rest of life is
  worth seeing //
within my mind every twist feels like the ride's
  careening.

If patterns arise then it coincides with lesson investing.
Saturn would rather move aside as a challenge to read
  between the lines,
as it matters if you're accepting of caressing.
The hammer drops from 888 million miles apart, I'd
  rather die
than admit that I might've been the guy who needed
  self-respect.

Perseverance is such a sexy phrase when all you've
  done is survive:
Yes, it takes strength; yes, it's brave; yes, it's better to
  be alive.

If you had never seen the light, because you've never
    had the time
to look up with present mind, admire the brightest sight –
mirrored in kind is the consequence of how "you" see
    "I".

I might've lied about what I felt inside, what's worse, is
    I also believed it.
The planet's fall and rise over our heads, beneath the
    heavens,
inspires I to maintain discipline, live with no regrets,
and valid cry whether I'm sad or elated.

SOLITAIRE

Queen of Spades,
who effortlessly seizes the day
while sitting alone on the park bench.
She's slicing the tattered deck
with riveting tales bestowed to those who listen.
How long has she sat atoned?
Does she even answer the rotary phone?
Delicately she places down
every card to complete the crown.

CHIRON

Chaos Theory permits that everything can happen
from a glance, a laugh, support, to turning back.
It's sutured up, the wounds that take time to fade
as we fell into disarray and all the light blackened.

 The question became: is this an attempt to
    communicate?
Isn't it twisted when the best intentions are laid to rest.
God was there, but I didn't take the bait.
"You had to grieve over and over for them," said the
    therapist.

I thought you drowned in a sea of confusion,
I dreamt you fell from a skyscraper to the frown.
I could tell that you wore perfume for someone else,
jealousy is a malicious lie we convince ourselves to go
    around.
If I had known the lengths you'd gone, they would've
    called me Confucious.
I at least knew you could climb the high ground.

Insanity said, "it isn't worth the risk,"
"reality's in shambles, scrambled by the end of whisk."
Love or run – is there really much of a difference?
I couldn't tell if it was self-love or diffidence.

ACT V:
THE HEART

HONESTY IS POLICY

Like many of you, in my youth, I was
isolated from the life outside and potential affection.
In my efforts to halt this mind and control my direction,
I filled the void with sex, substance addiction,
self-deprecation to mask my inhibitions.

The pattern emerges when I least expect it,
not because I stopped or conducted self-reflection.
I was never hated – no one had a reason to imagine
I would struggle with such anxiety and indecision.
It became insane since we mirrored deficient.

You concurred with complicity – a career in our magic.
You searched for simplicity, although it is tragic
at that point I detached from reality, I became enigmatic
in the place I once cherished, despite the love, I walked
    past it:
You call my name and all I hear is static.

Indirect jealousy, demanding free therapy, refusing to
    change
because – I fell into misery on purpose
instead of speaking up, breaking the charade.
I went from heights to accept I was in disarray.

Over and over, what could I have said to reconnect?
    The thought of honesty was rejected.
I am human, but I thought I had to be perfect //
and instead allowed you to escape, leaving me without
    a trace.

While you were still in my face. I believed myself to be
  a disgrace
and prayed to release you to save us all from my
  deranged.

Rehabilitate? Why didn't you give up until too late?
Didn't you see the implosion and give up the chase?
Instead of rummaging in the past, flipping the situation
  in every way,
I chose to let it go – forgive myself and reopen the
  garden gates.
Go forth today with intent.

BEATS PER MINUTE

Let your feet float off the ground, give yourself to
   the sound
of a million tiny heartbeats drifting endlessly.
Take a breath or count to ten, do whatever will help
   you Zen
as we walk the Garden of Michoacán.
If ten thousand thunder bugs did all sorts of crazy
   drugs
that would be one hell of a light show, wouldn't it?
Come lie back on the grass as your fears come to pass
just like grubs that aren't trapped.
Open up, please don't be shy, it's alright if you cry;
we're all just butterflies trying to connect.
The music between my ears hasn't sung in several
   years,
but it chimes aloud when you're around.
Step out of the chrysalis, let the words leave your lips
As I hang on every bit.
Their wings barely make a sound, too loud now turn
   it down,
I didn't hear what you just said.

TIRST

I should have given you flowers,
provide what you need to feel empowered //
I hang from grape vines turned sour,
in an act of defiance, down came the tower.

I love you so much it burns,
I wonder if you'll return.
Where should I search? Do you prefer a pool or a
   perch?
What time is your birth? Does she fill you with mirth?

If by putting you first, I let worse get to worst //
My cup runneth empty, I know you are tirst.
Your intentions are justified, why be honest
when I could just hide. It's been a difficult ride
for the one who makes you ignite.

Limits, boundaries unidentified //
Take any piece of me, I don't mind.
Please stay the night before
that version of me dies inside.

I'm the wild pariah, tell
your heart: do not let me inside them.
Showing up is a pact between friends,
in my state, how could I forget.

ROSEBUD

Even though thorns ruled her persona,
blossoming within the winter chamber
demonstrated her tremendous power.
Even so, it's blasphemous to forget
that she preferred luscious tulips
unlike what's called on first take.
I'd imagine the heavy, felled snowflake
didn't accept what she'd dictate,
but nonetheless, I will attest,
I think of her at every florist.

CALLIGRAPHY

If I could see,
I'd read the manuscripts
transferred from your mind to me,
not receipts from a former creed.
Vibrating rhymes shimmer similarly on the line,
an instant, a lonely point in time
where I tremble as reality trembles back in kind.
Now I feel it in my knees, a siren's nest to scheme
a bad religion to listen
who am I to dream?
Who could never triumph over sea,
the demon that drowns men beneath the sheen?
Only a solid home, shelter, and stone
a beaming lighthouse is enough light for me.
I see them still: green sails, blue trees, cool hills.
They're a sunflower warrior, a rocky-rose shore
  metaphor,
an oracle's sword, life breathes through her core.

TORRENT

I sleep better when it pours,
patters on the roof, so my soul can absorb.
Whether it's natural or a song on machine,
the thundering audio keeps me adream.

I won't stroll outside,
can't control the peeping sunlight.
Before the rays even break through,
I've memorized the movement to hit snooze.

Sometimes in the summer
I think aloud about the blunders,
of the above angels splitting 7-10,
and how they'll get there in the end.

NO CARDIGANS

Stubby little legs
that can't walk very far.
I don't always beg,
except to get in the car.
Short hair with honey amber,
I provide you all with only laughter.
Come closer, let's go, get after,
the naps are better without the fabric.
You know you can't ever complain,
I've outgrown all the stains.
Sure, it's another life to help forge,
but what else can you expect from a corgi.

BUT DON'T SEE ME

Fuck in the morning,
fuck all night –
perform everything that feels so right.
Add fuel to the fire,
teeth lie with desire,
mired from the DM gone quiet.

It came for the state //
Babe, let's repopulate,
intimacy's dead, but the money's not cringe,
I'll pay for a Mars trip instead.

Banned from the masses:
Rated "Red" for the asses
to dismantle the classes
that dispatch polite from crass.

   Woo!

It never hit like this!
We match Christian risks
right of the subliminal sticks,
no tricks, be vulnerable, safe and real.

Feel,
but don't see me.

COLD SCENES

A ballerina with deficient score
twirls alone at night,
roots patter on the tundra.
Her glow has left amends,
just as the solstice dreads
the spotlight that burns instead.
Whistle from across the rink,
step through the snow, implore some more
for her shimmering crime,
to swan dive beneath the light,
shattering the mirrors' plight
and disappeared out of sight.

FORWARD

Before the hour can collapse,
before Time wants investment back,
before my screen was ever cracked,
before my memories relapse,
I'm reminded of the rendezvous
against the will of the established path.
Whose courage flows with the wrath
of each step, forbidden by the breath,
as frost descends from summer's grasp,
the seeds of heel, from which I plant,
assure I'll find my way back
or forward, propelled from ripened snack.

WHISPER

Why does he close his eyes
every time he whispers?
"I love the way you're surprising
with your seething shimmer.
To pretend you glow enough
with what little light refracts,
you're just a stone's throw
from signing that contract."
He can't even remember
the last days of September,
let alone that we're not together.

MAYDAY

Liftoff //
because out in Texas
there's a high chance it'll turn sepsis.
Out in Georgia,
she'll be called a blasphemous whore.
In Idaho,
small towns see more than potatoes.

No matter how you spin it,
it's all about control.
A beat for delivery
pre- or post-partum,
only the mother can choose
to accept that from the bank or baby.

As I transition from lover to fighter –
heart once tight now overflows as courier –
I'll instead greet her at the blue border
and guide her to the best doctor.[17]

[17]Ever since Roe v. Wade was overturned in 2022, laws banning or restrict-ing abortion have gravely affected women across the country. The ruling has impacted access to lifesaving medical care, community resources, and safe abortions.
National Domestic Violence Hotline: (800) 799-7233.

ORPHEUS

At what cost can I sit a little taller
when frost collects like springtime pollen?
Am I wrong to assume
those muted reds bleed bluish hues?

Tell me how can Dionysus
strike poised like a desert dweller in disguise
Between the grape vines and cherry wine,
am I blind or does that shadow lie?

I'm moving too fast, dear Poison Pout
I don't know if my legs can last.
If the Sergeant of Arms won't twist me out,
then stamina carry me up the pass.

So close to Earth, I feel victory on my skin,
I glance behind only to ruin everything.
"Grab hold! Let me eclipse!" I exclaim
as the light burns my love slow and quick.
"Oh Orpheus," from phantom tongue and lips,
the Sun has reclaimed the candle stick.

THE CLONE

You look the same as me
from chiseled legs, speckled teeth,
the gentle huff when you breathe,
an unfamiliar, mirror copy.

You know all the roads
that led to here, the overgrown,
the hesitations, the decisive choices, to
remember the gaps in each other's memories.

It's like a game to find any imperfection
as we dance the same performance
like a phantom on the sidewalk.
Which of us took the first step?

MISSED CONNECTION

How do you catch up when it's terminal?
I have to carry on
dragging this baggage behind me,
gagging on the sliding sidewalk:
it's too straight forward to be a labyrinth.

I look outside at the airplanes taking off and crossing by,
I wonder if my flight ever even arrived.
Peering the scrolling screen of useless names:
Havana, New York, and Paris may be late.
How little time do I have?

I grip my tripod luggage
as the damned gatekeeper informed me of their
   departure.
Still in disbelief, I watch it taxi across the floor,
took off during a thunderstorm and disappeared from
   sight.
I guess that's better than a grounded flight.

OCTOBER

My position as the Owl holds honor and a scowl.
Within the roof of an forgotten day, another night
   against the grain,
mice frolic about the fields as true instincts are
   revealed.
An owl wise in shrouded disguise slips silently in the
   bind.
The mice are wary- blind but not mechanic.

The catch in my fist disappeared in a wisp
as the Raven neared – crisp and bold – a molten twist
for her nightly trip between the leaves of feathery kin.
The Raven rides with scythe in skin- sinister levels to
   the grin -
landing silently on my shore, a twig between us and
   nothing more.

The Raven rests beside my seat, I wince in the absence
   of the heat
"A clever treat," the stranger implored with nothing but
   a scorn.
What boar does this shadow take me for? Skeptical, I
   ask for more,
"Another night to explore" was all the Raven could
   export.
Yet there we sat, birds on a bench with unspoken word.

LOYALTY

I'm not brave
but I'm far from weak,
I'd gladly start a war for some sweets.
What's cowardly with enough care?
So you gotta save them,
You from you, tie your shoe,
release the sage and blow your rage,
take all that fury to therapy.

Who's not brave?
It depends on the week.
Who wouldn't start a fight just to see
if you love someone? How could that be?
It's not great for them to save you,
themselves from you, to cut you loose.
How do you gauge if you're safe
enough to have a burial at sea.

PENELOPE

I should have stayed
in the place I know I'm safe.
Instead, I played
in the sand where you remain
under our umbrellas.
Sorry if I kept you awake.

Oh, the shade,
I wish I stayed in the arms of the one that I love,
sipping the coconuts that fall from above.
Instead, I pulled a total Rover
by chasing the Sun, endless pursuit
with plenty of fun.
Then the tide pulled me away.

Away,
Inside I suffocated
knowing that you're patient and
with uncertain expectations,
wouldn't mind the distance.
But FaceTime doesn't exist yet,
so I cry over sundried crustaceans
and navigate with constellations
just to be back with you.

CASSIOPEIA

Queen Cassiopeia talks to you sweet, stars on a stormy
    sea,
sailors follow her home - her job is never over -
she ever had time to be alone or
yearn for that sun-kissed sand home.
What can they even see?

On the horizon the lighthouse pierces through
open sea for any ship or sinking soul too.
Rooted in his duty, commanding admirals few,
King Pisces, slipping back above the gleam,
what's a storm to he?

From the roost atop the tallest sail, he
finds the eye of a nebula most divine,
who shone a light and prevailed with all her might,
they admired how well it ignited.

ASPEN HEIGHTS

What's the rush for Colorado?
We can take our time as each season rolls by,
we've got beaches, the jelly sand, lemonade in the
  summertime
East Coast Primetime, mornings hunting us through the
  blinds.
You thrive in the sunlight, so why can't you wait?
We put in effort till our shoes hurt,
till our arms break, it's a give and take.
We don't know how far back the Woodlands go
but I got gas in case you wanna roam.
I know nothing's all right, is there something to fight?
Someone can't even play the game right.
We were so far away, weaving between lanes.
We can't sleep in, I'll remember which pillow has your
  name.

FANCY MOTORCARS

I'm not like those other guys with fancy motorcars.
Tell me darling how'd you get those scars?
I'm not your boy but I can be your friend,
you're not a toy to be broke or bent.
Like when they tell you you're special as a dazzling
   light,
like a flower kind or when something's in your eye,
before the crash and inferno like a fancy motorcar.
I for one am guilty of the very same crime,
but taking chances on others is how we even got this far
because the human inside you is something utterly
   divine.

SPACE RACE

We made a little bet – a promise if you will –
to see which one of us could forget the insanity
of earthly desires before the other, as gravity
demands that we stay still.

I began to dance for a little chance
of overcoming this insatiable,
perplexing trap we found ourselves in.
Alongside me, you laughed and pranced
and embraced the law of supernatural,
and I witnessed you float for more than a second.

Then we leapt, as sure as the Moon
crept across our field of view,
neither of us grew tired or content
or at least we pretended to.

It took all our individual might
to stay in the atmosphere, cast away
from irritants and city lights,
until our fingers tangled and strayed
the safety of each other's embrace.
Love remains in the reflection of your face.

IN REVERSE

I can say it, I have the heart.
On the last day, at the first hour,
assessed hard feelings to prosper.
We ride, you navigate until dawn,
we take turns choosing songs to fawn,
sharing laughter, structures above flowing water,
distance traversed in the blink of an eye,
with hands unclasped so I could drive.
The remaining time was less sublime,
bickering on backroads, a clear highway,
"I know where to go, we follow the signs,"
 And that didn't stop me from pondering.
You were still inquisitive,
we went far, covered many miles.
as anyone expected,
We fell apart.
[Now, read line-by-line backwards]

MATRIMONY

We're gathered here, dearly beloved
to witness the matrimony
between Gold Fist and Velvet Glove,
sanctioned by Thucydides -
surrounded by lovers and strangers,
objective haters, life savers, and
chirpings from loose aunties,
who all watch from different cities –
praying to God it's nothing but fog,
there's not enough rain for us to delay
this combination any farther.
Where's the flower boy? Did he
skip town with the priestess of high order?
No matter, the show must go on,
let's jig a dance and sing a song
until we forget what planet we're from.

ACT VI:
THE WORLD

ODE TO NATION-BUILDING

The candle can possess many names:
hope, promise, compassion, death, ambivalence, shame.
The smoke will dance on the waxed grave,
a shell of the life now separated.

Now there's room for a new flame –
the one sparked out of desperation
to keep harsh memories ablaze.
You whispered with eyes affixed to the membrane
weaved to keep the charcoal in place:
"We will rebuild better. God believes in the forsaken."

Then the artists came, when once cast aside by the
    standardized.
Then the architects arrived, with plans that stretch
    beyond the sky.
Then the neighbors brought supplies left from foreign
    infections.
Then you, who bared the torch through the very cavern,
    led division to unify.
Then, as the weeks shift and plans laid deliberate,
    questions still lingered:
"How do we move on? Why even bother? What
    tomorrow do we solidify?"

They already plundered, ravaged, and failed to conquer,
every home is battered and heartbroken.
These bricks will remain, left unbothered
until it's agreed how they're carried forward.
Those damn liberators returned with better vision,
offered help, accepted the declination, and left a

beachbound gift
of hammers, masonry, finances, and note of
   proclamation:
"We understand. Please do with this how you wish."

In the success of reinstitution comes the greater
   challenges:
to reconcile history, relinquish inequality, redistribute
   resources,
rekindle a constitution and reinvigorate the masses.
They come with a cost foreseen by scales
balanced with affectionate, accessible ballots
for every one heart and thought.

It can be fixed over nights, in hand
with the hope of growing this fertile land.
Eventually, after progressing so many yesterdays,
all descendants have a place to stay.[18]

[18]Inspired by a 2008 speech by Ibrahim Gambari on the challenges of
nation-building in Nigeria – who at the time, served as the Under Secre-
tary-General of the United Nations for Political Affairs.

ANOTHER TRAVERSER

Please just take it with you.
I know you know what to do
when you get to the rendezvous:
you'll have in both headphones
stare out the window,
watching tall fields as they wave past,
endless terrain as the sky turns brass,
experience good news when you arrive exactly
when the good Lord had asked.

Call me when you get there,
text me if you can't chat,
remember to send the signal
if you won't turn back.
I'll be on the next flight out
to catch you before the land.

PENANCE OF ISAAC

The hand that wields the knife
understands its many, troubled lives.
It will cut, carve, iinsurrect and feed
on the survival of eternity required to breed.
This is not its own decision –
as the hand commands each slice
of their very volition.
Perhaps a surgical scalpel has an opinion
that differs from the slender scimitar.
Which am I: the hand or the knife?
I read, I consume, I explore, and I produce,
as destiny keeps me blind to the truth.
I will not suffer should the second blade
return to bite this hand.
Its nature is fluid, solidified by intent.
As am I, as I enjoy the apple with history.

I AM HERE

The first ones to go
are those unable to defend
against the system they depend upon.
Unless the body you've grown
is prime – whatever that intends –
the people who live and cannot pretend
to be scarce, are instead controlled through genetics.

Shoutout JR:
the man who rose for them all,
because you do hear them when they call.
Dowsed before others are made divisible,
they're canaries for when everything falls.

Disabled folks deserve a seat at the table //
Say it:
"I belong here because I am capable."[19]

[19]Historically, people with disabilities – whether due to physical or mental conditions – are left out of conversations across institutions. From systemic barriers in healthcare to education to careers, having access to basic needs met becomes ever more challenging.

INVINCIBLE

I can suspend my stride
above the gaze of city lights.

I see serenity so close
yet out of reach, only
complacency as the tide
goes rolling,
rolling onward.

How this approach breathes form
for fellow Mercurian ghosts,
I don't know.

I have certainty, that if I fall,
you'll drag and sprawl your arms to catch me –
catch me before I contrarily thought.

WHAT THEY WOVE IN US

There once lived four sisters:
Cece, Vava, Jojo, and Ziti.

Cece always had the certain soup and bread galore,
who chose to hand-wring laundry well into century
   21,
alone in her creaky, Brooklyn home.

Vava clung to the beach, pried every mollusk
her husband would retrieve,
forever peachy and sweet.

Jojo had that laugh that echoed
throughout the nights,
considerate of the many plights.

Ziti, the youngest with spit aflame,
had saint's patience and simmered
until she left for the hereafter.

I knew of the former two, who
held my mother close, even cusped 100
when her Ziti went to rest.

The four wove through my family tree
with full love, faithful woes,
kindness extravagant, and clear conscience.

For those, and for their surviving strength,
I wonder how they now gaze on the holy quilt
that we cannot appreciate from below.

FISSURE

I wish shackles spoke
with less volition.
The stories they would tell
over the centuries, over the last few days.

It's been so long since
the last reset.
I wish I could stay here,
just to chalk down
another broken record
maybe the reward's to blame.

No hotel could keep me for very long,
they're built up just to be unsung.
I spy between the loosest links
that freedom is a clank away.

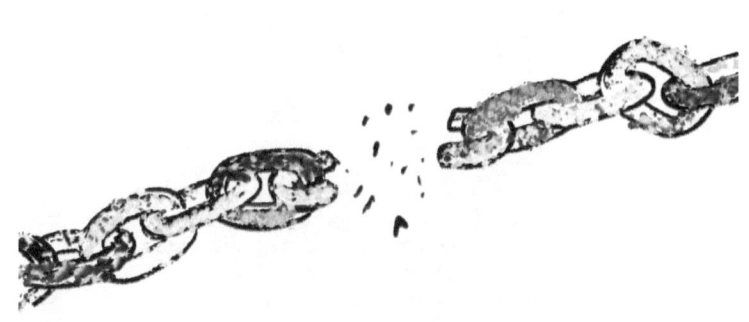

TIN-CAN DRUMS

So what if I'm made of stardust?
It's not like that'll remove the rust
from these tin-can drums I bang
every day so I can afford some lunch.

Who cares if I've gone astray?
I play during each heat wave
and sleet paved streets
that become stronger by the rotate.

The passerby politicians still say,
while entering gated estates:
"Don't pretend like you had no choice,
your music plays for held rejoice."

It's true, I'm a little bit blue,
does systemic support mean something to you?
But if your son smiles during this tattered song,
then you tell him which one of us is wrong.[20]

---

[20]According to the Economic Policy Institute, inequality in the US reached record highs during the COVID-19 pandemic, as the richest 10% of Americans possess over 90% of the total stock market. Corporations have steadily undermined workers' rights for decades, reinforcing an oligarchy through massive transfers of wealth and the lack of consensus on how to hold them accountable.
According to the US Department of Housing and Urban Development (HUD), individuals experiencing homelessness rose 18% to 770,000 between 2023 and 2024, with a worsening pace as inequality grows.

IMMOLATION

I cast no shadow as I stride today.
What more can I say?
Under the circumstance,
my mind still entranced by
reeling wheels, I'm ready to collapse.
I'll rhyme, I'll spit poetry and dance,
shiver at the end of the last act.
My knees may buckle, I'm still alive.
I try to stand; some say to survive.
I rise with all my might,
nothing can douse my light //

Bushnell, Bruce, Buckel, Bouazizi[21]

[21]In April 2024, US Air Force Airman Aaron Bushnell committed self-immo-
lation in protest of Israeli actions against Palestinians. He was 25 years old.
On Earth Day, 2022, climate activist and Buddhist Wynn Alan Bruce
ignited outside of the US Supreme Court in protest of the government's
inaction to climate change. He was 50.
In April 2018, David Buckel was an LGBT rights lawyer remembered for
his work at Lambda Legal, and on his victories in Nabozny v. Podlesny
and Brandon v. County of Richardson. He was 60.
In December 2010, Tunisian street vendor Mohammed Bouazizi lit himself
on fire in protest of an oppressive, corrupt system, catalyzing the Jasmine
Revolution and what would be known as the Arab Spring. He was 26.

DOOM

From once upon this rock,
body shackled, left to rot,
to rest, weary from the clock,
I lie without a line to cross.

Sudden cracks in the fabric
of neither false nor true,
one second of panic
preceded by vibrant purple feuds.

Where I once flopped, exalted nonetheless,
and for my fall, I will attest,
in the hour of my wickedness
I too fell victim, in my own protest.

Where I went, you unfortunately can't relate
to the dreamlike state that I fabricate.
My eyes still shutter and quake,
now unbound, I am awake.

SUPERPOSITION

Let's hear it for the maestro!
They're 300 years ahead from humanity's low,
the sonic waves that cluster and brine
from dusk until the morning rise.

But lo! Has this orchestra atoned?
What began will end in Europa, distant ice and stone,
from both our home on Gaia and Jupiter's Godly Eye,
that decide if the enemy is worth it this time.

I am here – ready to defend the colonies of a far
off land. It's intergalactic – this plague of human –
who now traverse planets as one from work to the bar.
If we are still exploited thousands of years after the
    Mayan's ruin,
by systems that refused to address their scars,
it is safe to say that the violence will endure and
    sustain.

One worldly revolt sparks another, then another, then
    another,
until the entire solar neighborhood is up in flames.
War, unlike anything we can dream or conjure
from forgotten people, raging machines, and indistinct
    creatures.
If it exists, I cannot do as I wish. I refuse to give it a
    name
at risk that this equality will inspire roaring change.

THE BALLAD OF ICARUS

Crete is no haven for a deity
nor is Olympus for a mortal.
An eye blind to glimpse history
leaves man's struggle eternal.

Daedalus, father of innovation,
Benevolent Superego,
challenges the stature of the divine,
condemning his son to soar like stone.

With arms outstretched they'll take to the skies.
An act obscene: bold and unholy,
insomniac-riddled fireflies,
damned wings beat at the spark of light.

Icarus, fledgling to the matador,
a fools' dove who pursues Apollo's tail
and falls before the comet ablaze.
He crumbles, his feathers refused to sail.

Daedalus – fights a bull for any man -
weeps for irksome gods and thunderclaps,
watches grinned Icarus crumbled to the sea below
and pierced upon the dreaded trident.

PRINCE WINTER

Purity drifting from oblivion,
the taste of sour on my tongue,
I wander the tundra of good intentions,
a fitting price for the grudge.

My heels fell numb before the toes,
each step plunging back in cold.
Out here, there is no other foe,
my companion is a man of old.

I came across an impasse of sorts,
there was no sign or fork in road.
A sensation guides me without force,
does this mean I've reached my goal?

Is that a flame between the grey?
The dance appears so regal.
If true, I'll bargain for a stay,
a glowing bed has no equal.

Energy surges in my lungs
to propel me to the shelter.
If my lips moved, I'd have sung
a tune to keep me warmer, yet
I collapse long after winter stung.
If my hand could reach, I'd tell them.

KRÁSNÝ SVĚT

Havel said:
Hope is the circumstance
within the human heart
that we are bound to believe
the complexities of society
can swell our spirits
in the harshest time.

To demoralize this conundrum -
in the hour of paradox
where meaning recedes
and life is dwarfed
by rabid tarantism –
to forfeit your inspiration
will yield to malice complacency.

When Velvet calls
for our worldly reunion,
when peace reigns supreme,
and violence fears rescindment,
the power of democracy
and death of bureaucracy
will finally join hands.[22]

[22]The Velvet Revolution of 1989 began as a primarily student-led, peaceful protest against Soviet authoritarianism. Led by playwright-dissident Václav Havel (1936 – 2011), the movement succeeded in a non-violent transition of power and subsequent independence of Czechoslovakia.

QUANTUM

I'm certain that poetry –
of which, can encapsulate all art –
is nothing more, nothing less,
than personified quantum mechanics.
I ask you to consider this:
simply observing the atomic particle
interjects with its reality.
We see the stubborn atom –
microscopic, morphing, and metabolizing –
only by position or trajectory,
although never simultaneous.

What defines creativity?
The effortful skill, ham-fisted ambiguousness,
a relative flow, preposterous allegory,
that savored emotion it inhibits?
All, I argue, are true.
Perhaps it's fresher perception
that defines a classic, static masterpiece.
Perhaps the magical Artist
breathes life into the inanimate.
Perhaps I'm curious
to hear a critique of the next da Vinci.
Perhaps, like the atom everywhere,
it's best to interpret
at the moment in time
or in the path of retrospect.

WEEKEND AFTER

I didn't come just to fit in,
the stool's the perfect height
so I can see above the curtailed remorse
as blinding lights reflect on the dance floor.
I don't see my friends yet, maybe they'll arrive
after I spend some time mesmerized by
the maligned vision of shammy eyeliner.
The venue's too big, instincts set to flee or fight.
You said you're only spending the night
and won't take my money, it doesn't seem right.
I still haven't spent my entire paycheck,
it's not much, but enough to get me spinning.
I think this is the part where I should have fun,
the tab's not closed, fill this and make it a double.
I'm not looking for trouble, keep its name out of
    your mouth.
As alone and so below, dressed to impress no
    one,
I'll gladly take your ass down.

IRON LUNG

The air cannot be still, it froths with each exhale.
Comrades, take one step further down,
the canaries sing and never frown.
Lead is crumbs, I remember the trillionth
time I was stung. Still I work until the chime
of the dinner bell being rung.

Uncle Sam has done us proud,
now we won't see those thunderclouds.
But how am I supposed to throw a party,
let alone go home to see my daughter properly?

The question is the pressure,
I wouldn't say if I didn't know better.
I suggest befriending the abyss,
you'll be lucky to see the surface again.

I didn't sign up for this!
I demand another chance,
I can't be Odysseus!
I think of all the things that I miss,
I still need to scold my baby after her first kiss.

Attention! Code Red! Listen to the radio!
The birds have stopped chirping,
The men fall like dominos!
Get down below your knees,
pray that it's caught on video!

ABUNDANT WAR

Factories – designed to streamline each
stroke of inspired folk – progress the
endless stream of toy soldiers who hesitate
on the front lines, their thoughts scheme:

"Dying to retreat, my family at home needs
me to purge vicious interlopers from
foreign, soiled beachhead. Packaged,
labeled, serial shipped to cry havoc in unison
in some strange village, this joint pillage
of those homes ahead of me.
One more battle until I see them again.
Again, only one fray remains."

Tomorrow only comes for the ones
required by Will of Wrath, to remember
their face as if neighbor carries their name,
as all involved pray the next war
never sees the light of day.
Remains – like scurried, soiled boot–
often stay buried in place.[23]

---

[23] According to the Washington Post, the United States has reportedly inter-
vened in the governments of 72 nations – most notably in Latin America
and Southeast Asia. A majority of regime changes resulted in destabilized
regions and systemic human rights violations, ultimately in favor of Amer-
ican corporations.

CAMBODIAN EGO DEATH

The first five pages were written in the middle row,
the stewardess even asked to dim the laptop glow.
I sighed, but recognized the creativity needed to expand,
the spark can wait until after we land.
No window nearby – I couldn't look outside – but the
young family across the aisle were having a delight.
I'm no soldier; freedom is my only friend.
The longer I held onto that triviality,
the less time I had until the peanuts send.

I somehow wrote far more in that far-flung endeavor:
a guest house sitting by the Mekong River.
This is too conceded, I've gotta clean the deep end,
I sat alone at the ramen shop, relieved that
that loneliness is a share curse. I forget if
localized craft beer was something to regret,
but buying one for them to become your bud.
I'll admit, it gave me ample motivation
to accept that chance of rebirth.

THE EIFFEL

Excuse me Doctor, I know I'm holding you late,
but procedures haven't been all that cheap or great.
Why am I soft in the middle when my life is so hard?
There were plenty hints of allegations – sorry, I should
    let you exhale.
I'm usually less stressed when this cigarette turns pale.

He said: "This isn't a cathedral, should I call the
    preacher?
I've been looking after people all day as if there's a
    serial freak
or someone else to blame. I've seen when legacies in
    peril
turn overcooked, blanketed in novocaine apparel.
You'll cough first; I know the smoke seems delightful,
an orchestra must repose before their recital:
I alone can't carry you down from the Eiffel."

It sounds too easy to claim your decisions,
I've been told not to let the Seine turn brittle.
Still waters run familiar, so what's your conviction?
Did you fall in love in this biological kitchen?
My mission was never to isolate or neglect
all the people who said they're ready to forget.

"You're right, and it's not like I can admit
that with consideration, heartfelt persistence, that
every problem you face would suddenly extinguish.
What I will say, and this I can attest,
trust that you're supported and travel if you wish.
It's a harsh life that the catacombs demand,
but it gets much easier when you hold someone's hand."[24]

[24]National Suicide Prevention Lifeline: 988. You deserve to be loved and appreciated.

JANUS THE GATEKEEPER

I haven't earned the worth, know
before our time here expires:
I peered through the keyhole //
saw Autumn Pillars
with throne left vacant, exposed,
marble floors so clerical,
I am clearly the inheritable regal.
C'mon, rose vines reach heavens higher,
as time is slipping shorter,
distorting my temper.
Your door, creaking history,
beard disheveled with amnesty,
shall I offer a challenge coin?
This shouldn't be my burden,
the riches laugh in sinister,
you've grown so much darker.
Sunlight bleeds further into night,
Fate is here with End in sight,
I guess we can dance
and twirl in the eternal moonlight.

EVEREST

Midnight Dream
blessing me with her highest peak.
It looks easy, but her job is never clean,
to command constellations so sailors can see.
Endless friends yet she feels alone,
can someone else rule the throne?

Mourning June arrives on time,
bitter warmth hugs the mountain blight.
As Day climbs, the World glows, Night evaporates,
the spotlight seeps in every crack and feature,
through rock roses and sleet creatures.
Flint inspired jungle fever; she melts his desires
 to finally catch fire.

She only sees an empty road, down the slope lies the
 globe
Still she can't let go, she wants to stay untouchable.
On cue the cold erodes, daybreak's might to behold.
Night resides as Day arrives, together they explore the
 cosmos.

ERASING THE USURPER

There's passion in your heart.
I can see it
in the way you signed your name
on the bottom right corner of your desires.
How diligently you focused the calligraphy
for your masterpiece
birthed out of anxiety.

I feel it
in your attention to detail
as you probably spent days, weeks even,
perfecting the paint strokes:
the canvas, desolate //
the crown, jagged //
the wolf, ravenous.

I listen
to the nervous handshake,
the compassionate eyes,
and eager mind.
Thank you
for sharing this with me.[25]

---

[25] An artist I met in college inspired me to write this – their heartfelt creativity can be seen in so many others and should always be cherished.

FIRST BASTION

I envy finality, the closing of stories that
we admire and fear - ideally one will disappear.
To regard this merely as misconstrued, rather
than spending specter seconds fraying tooth,
on surface can blossom with righteous intent
as the individual resides in devil's grip.

To be blessed as Last is to persevere with honor
rid of such besmirch, compared to neighbor's falter.
Ferocious, again erupts the men, women, child akin
inspired by echoed words: "the torch still endures!"
However, should the flame truly sputter out,
then the worst endeavor is over now.

Never diminish me to this: as if millions
more aren't capable of sweeter bliss.
The turret, restored from abandoned, budding field,
once forgotten by order of Stolen Seal, relinquished
from shackles which held this life besieged, exclaims
    today:
"I am the First Bastion, as the catalyst clearly believed."

REFERENCES

Blair, Hunter. "It's Not Trickling down: New Data Provides No Evidence That the TCJA Is Working as Its Proponents Claimed It Would." Economic Policy Institute, July 29, 2019. https://www.epi.org/blog/its-not-trickling-down-new-data-provides-no-evidence-that-the-tcja-is-working-as-its-proponents-claimed-it-would/.

"Firearms Are the Leading Cause of Death for Children and Teens in the US." Everytown Research & Policy, 8 Nov. 2024, http://everytownresearch.org/graph/firearms-are-the-leading-cause-of-death-for-american-children-and-teens/

Gambari, Ibrahim A. "The Challenges of Nations Building: The Case of Nigeria." Abuja, Nigeria: Mustapha Akanbi Foundation, 2008. https://www.mafng.org/anniversary/challenges_nation_building_nigeria.htm

Herman, Edward S., and Noam Chomsky. Manufacturing Consent the Political Economy of the Mass Media Edward S. Herman ; Noam Chomsky. Pantheon, 2002.

"HUD Releases January 2024 Point-in-Time Count Report: Hud. Gov / U.S. Department of Housing and Urban Development (HUD)." HUD Releases January 2024 Point-In-Time Count Report | HUD.Gov / U.S. Department of Housing and Urban Development (HUD), http://www.hud.gov/press/press_releases_media_advisories/hud_no_24_327#:~:text=The%20report%20found%20more%20than,given%20changed%20policies%20and%20conditions

"James Baldwin - The Artist's Struggle for Integrity (Full Recording)." YouTube video, 3:45, "-stella-," July 23, 2015. https://www.youtube.com/watch?v=dU0g5fAA2QY&t=227s

Killelea, Steve. "Over one billion people at threat of being displaced by 2050 due to environmental change, conflict and civil unrest." London, United Kingdom: Institute for Economics & Peace, 2020. https://www.economicsandpeace.org/wp-content/uploads/2020/09/Ecological-Threat-Register-Press-Release-27.08-FINAL.pdf.

O'Rourke, Lindsey A. "Analysis | the U.S. Tried to Change Other Countries' Governments 72 Times during the Cold War." The Washington Post. WP Company, December 7, 2021. https://www.washingtonpost.com/news/monkey-cage/wp/2016/12/23/the-cia-says-russia-hacked-the-u-s-election-here-are-6-things-to-learn-from-cold-war-attempts-to-change-regimes/.

Statistics about Sexual Violence, https://www.nsvrc.org/sites/default/files/publications_nsvrc_factsheet_media-packet_statistics-about-sexual-violence_0.pdf..

"The Ten Stages of Genocide." Holocaust Memorial Day Trust, hmd.org.uk/learn-about-the-holocaust-and-genocides/what-is-genocide/the-ten-stages-of-genocide/.

United Nations High Commissioner for Refugees. "Frequently Asked Questions on Climate Change and Disaster Displacement." UNHCR, November 6, 2016. https://www.unhcr.org/uk/news/latest/2016/11/581f52dc4/frequently-asked-questions-climate-change-disaster-displacement.html.

ABOUT THE AUTHOR

Steven James Faviano (he/him) is a storyteller and humanitarian with a passion for exploring the human condition. A graduate of Florida State University, he had the opportunity to study human rights violations across Europe and Southeast Asia, experiences that deeply shaped his worldview. Since 2020, he has worked with local political campaigns, grassroots movements, and nonprofit organizations, dedicating his efforts to meaningful change.

As a writer, Steven relentlessly seeks out stories and unique perspectives, continually refining his understanding of the world. Recent years have shown that while humanity takes collective strides forward, we now find ourselves teetering on the edge of catastrophe. Though history offers lessons, we face an onslaught of new horrors that demand discernment and a renewed focus on class consciousness.

He believes that understanding how we arrived at this moment requires a critical reevaluation of the systems that govern us. To truly reclaim our dreams, we need a surge of creativity, empathy, and community-building. This book – like many before it – strives to illuminate this path forward.

www.ingramcontent.com/pod-product-compliance
Lightning Source LLC
Chambersburg PA
CBHW031524120626
46545CB00005B/1986